The Learning Works

Fearless Phonics

A Phonics Handbook
With Rules and Super Word Lists!

Written by Linda Schwartz • Illustrated by Bev Armstrong

The Learning Works

Fearless Phonics

A Phonics Handbook
With Rules and Super Word Lists!

Written by Linda Schwartz • Illustrated by Bev Armstrong

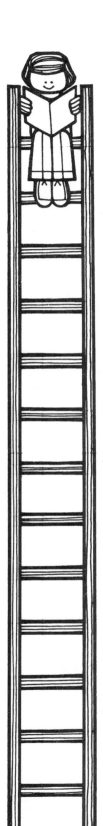

The Learning Works

Editing:
Linda Loeffler

Typography:
Kimberley A. Clark

A special thank you to Sonia Crestfied and Leslie Smith. Thanks also go to Colleen Solomon, Literacy Resource Teacher, Burbank Unified School District, in Burbank, California.

A Note to Teachers and Parents

Finally! A simple, hands-on resource unlocking the mysteries of phonics for teachers and parents working with children to help them master reading skills. According to AB 3482 California Readership Initiative materials, "Phonics is a way of teaching reading and spelling that stresses symbol-sound relationships." With the clear, easy-to-use approach presented in *Fearless Phonics*, students will learn to apply basic rules and eliminate guesswork from reading.

The first two sections, "Conquering Consonants" and "Vowel Victories," provide the keys for decoding most English words by associating sound with spelling. Generalizations, rules, and samples are included for blends, digraphs, diphthongs, and more.

The book also includes helpful lists such as basic sight words and rhyming word families, as well as commonly-used prefixes, suffixes, and roots, along with definitions and sample words.

Finally, students receive help with "Dividing Words Into Syllables and Marking Accents."

Because the basic generalizations and rules of phonics are between the covers of this book, you'll find yourself referring to it over and over again.

3

Contents

 **Conquering Consonants**

 Super Word Lists

 **Vowel Victories**

Dividing Words Into Syllables and Placing Accent Marks

Conquering Consonants

Fearless Phonics
© The Learning Works, Inc.

Consonants

Consonants are all the letters of the alphabet except the vowels **a,e,i,o,u**, and sometimes **y**. Although there are twenty-six letters in the English alphabet, there are 24 consonant sounds. Some consonant sounds are represented by a single letter, such as:

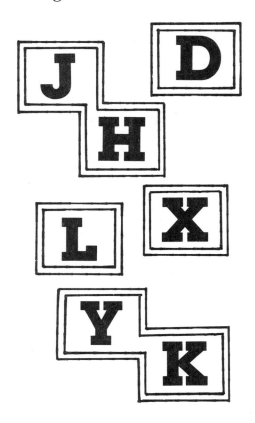

b as in boy
d as in do
f as in for
g as in go
h as in her
j as in jar
k as in kitten
l as in low
m as in man
n as in no
p as in pop
r as in ran
s as in so
t as in to
v as in van
w as in way
y as in you
z as in zebra

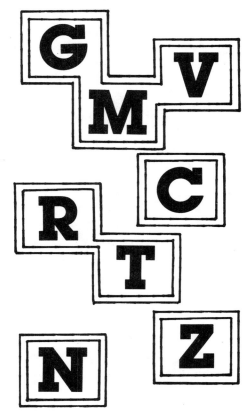

(The letters **c**, **q**, and **x** don't have distinct sounds of their own.) There are also some consonant sounds that use combinations of letters ("digraphs") rather than a single consonant. Here are some examples:

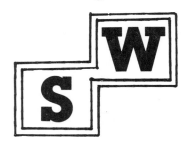

ch as in **ch**air
ng as in si**ng**
sh as in **sh**elf
th as in **th**ese

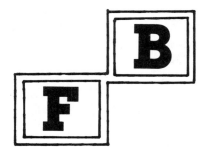

Consonant Blends

A *consonant blend* consists of two or more consonant sounds blended together where both sounds are heard distinctly, such as **blue**. Here are some common two-letter consonant blends: *bl, br, cl, cr, dr, fl, fr, gl, gr, pl, pr, sc, sk, sl, sm, sn, sp, st, sw, tr, tw* and *wh*.

bl	**br**	**cl**	**cr**
black	brace	claim	crab
blade	brag	clamp	crack
blame	braid	clang	craft
blank	brain	clap	crash
blanket	brake	clash	crate
blare	brand	clasp	crave
blast	brass	class	crawl
bleak	brawl	classic	crayon
bleed	bread	classify	craze
bless	break	claw	cream
blind	breed	clean	crease
blink	bribe	clear	creek
blip	brick	clerk	crest
bliss	bridge	cliff	crew
blister	brief	climb	crib
block	brim	clip	crisp
bloom	brink	clock	crook
blow	broad	close	crop
blue	broil	cloth	crow
bluff	brood	clown	crowd
blunt	brook	club	crumb
blur	brown	clumsy	crush
blush	brush	clutch	cry

7

Fearless Phonics
© The Learning Works, Inc.

Consonant Blends

dr	fl	fr	gl	gr
drab	flag	fraction	glad	grab
drag	flake	fragile	glade	grace
drain	flame	fragrant	glance	grain
drape	flannel	frail	gland	grand
draw	flare	frame	glare	grape
dread	flash	frank	gleam	graph
dream	flat	frantic	glee	grasp
drench	flaunt	fraud	glen	grass
dress	flavor	fray	glib	grate
dribble	flaw	freak	glide	grave
drift	flee	free	glimmer	graze
drill	fleece	freeze	glimpse	grease
drink	flex	fresh	glint	great
drip	fling	friend	glitch	greed
drive	flip	fright	glitter	grid
drivel	float	frizz	gloat	grief
drone	flood	from	glob	grill
drool	flop	frond	globe	grind
droop	florist	front	gloom	grip
drop	floss	frost	glop	grit
drown	flour	frown	glory	groan
drowsy	flower	frozen	gloss	ground
drug	flunk	frugal	glow	growl
drum	flute	fruit	glum	gruff
dry	fly	fry	glut	grunt

Consonant Blends

pl	pr	sc	sk
place	praise	scab	skate
placid	prance	scald	skeleton
plague	prank	scale	skeptic
plain	pray	scalp	sketch
plan	present	scalpel	skew
plane	press	scamp	ski
planet	pretty	scan	skid
plant	pretzel	scar	skill
plastic	preview	scarce	skim
plate	pride	scatter	skimp
platter	prime	scold	skin
play	print	scoop	skip
plead	prize	scope	skirt
please	product	scorch	skitter
plod	profit	score	skulk
plow	project	scorn	skull
plug	prom	scout	skunk
plum	prompt	scuff	sky
plunk	proof	sculptor	
plural	protect	scum	
ply	proud	scurry	

Fearless Phonics
© The Learning Works, Inc.

Consonant Blends

sl	sm	sn	sp	st
slab	smack	snack	space	stable
slack	small	snag	spade	stack
slam	smart	snake	span	staff
slang	smash	snap	spare	stair
slant	smear	snarl	spark	stake
slap	smell	snatch	sparrow	stale
slash	smile	sneak	speak	stall
slate	smock	sneeze	spear	stamp
slave	smog	sniff	speed	stand
sled	smoke	snip	spend	star
sleep	smooth	snob	spice	steal
slender	smug	snoop	spin	steel
slept		snore	spine	step
slick		snow	spirit	stew
slim		snub	spoil	still
sling		snug	spoke	sting
slope			spool	stitch
slow			spoon	stock
slug			sport	stool
slumber			spot	stop
slur			spud	story
sly			sputter	stub
			spy	student
				stun
				stupid

Consonant Blends

sw	tr	tw	wh
swaddle	trace	tweak	whale
swagger	track	twice	wharf
swap	trade	twig	what
swarm	traffic	twilight	wheat
swat	trail	twill	wheel
sway	tramp	twin	when
swear	trap	twine	where
sweat	travel	twinkle	whether
sweep	treat	twirl	which
sweet	trek	twist	while
swell	trench	twister	whine
swerve	trend	twitch	whip
swift	tribe	twitter	whirl
swim	trick		whisper
swirl	trim		whistle
swivel	trip		white
	truce		whiz
	truck		why
	trust		
	try		

11

Fearless Phonics
© The Learning Works, Inc.

Consonant Blends

Here are some common three-letter consonant blends.

sch	scr	spl	spr	str	tch	thr
schedule	scrap	splash	sprain	strain	catch	thrash
scheme	scrape	splatter	sprawl	strait	etch	threat
scholar	scratch	spleen	spray	strand	fetch	thresh
school	scrawl	splendid	spread	strange	latch	threw
schooner	scream	splendor	spree	strap	match	thrift
	screech	splice	sprig	straw	patch	thrive
	screen	splint	spring	stray	pitch	throat
	scroll	splinter	sprinkle	streak	snatch	throb
	scrub	splurge	sprint	stream	switch	through
			sprung	street	watch	thrust
			spry	stretch	wretch	
				strew		
				strict		
				strike		
				stripe		
				stroke		
				stroll		
				struggle		

Consonant Digraphs

A *consonant digraph* consists of two consonants that make up a single speech sound. Sometimes the consonant digraph appears at the beginning of a word.

ch	gh	gn	kn
change	ghastly	gnarly	knack
chap	ghetto	gnash	knave
check	ghost	gnat	knead
chill	ghoul	gnaw	knell
chimp		gneiss	knight
chop		gnome	knit
chug		gnu	know

ph	sh	th	wr
phantom	shady	thank	wrangle
phase	shed	the	wrath
pheasant	sheet	thick	wreck
phobia	shelf	thin	wrestle
phone	shift	this	wriggle
photo	ship	thumb	wring
physical	shop	thump	wrought

Fearless Phonics
© The Learning Works, Inc.

Consonant Digraphs

A *consonant digraph* consists of two consonants that make a single speech sound. Sometimes the consonant digraph appears at the end of a word.

ch	ck	ng	th
beach	back	bang	bath
bench	black	clang	booth
bunch	clock	hang	both
inch	deck	hung	cloth
lunch	flock	long	math
lurch	luck	rang	moth
peach	mock	rung	path
pinch	pick	sang	tooth
punch	quick	sing	truth
reach	rack	sung	with
teach	sock	thing	wrath

The /sh/ and /zh/ Sounds

Words that contain the consonants **t**, **s**, and **c** sometimes sound like **/sh/** or **/zh/** when followed by an **i** and another vowel.

ti	**si**	**ci**
ambition	mansion	facial
collection	mission	glacier
motion	session	musician
nation	tension	social
potential	vision	suspicion

15

Fearless Phonics
© The Learning Works, Inc.

Silent Consonants

Sometimes when two consonants are together, only the first consonant is heard and the second one is silent.

bo<u>m</u>b   la<u>m</u>b   <u>s</u>word

Other times, when two consonants are together, only the second consonant is heard and the first one is silent.

cal<u>f</u>   chal<u>k</u>   doub<u>t</u>   pal<u>m</u>

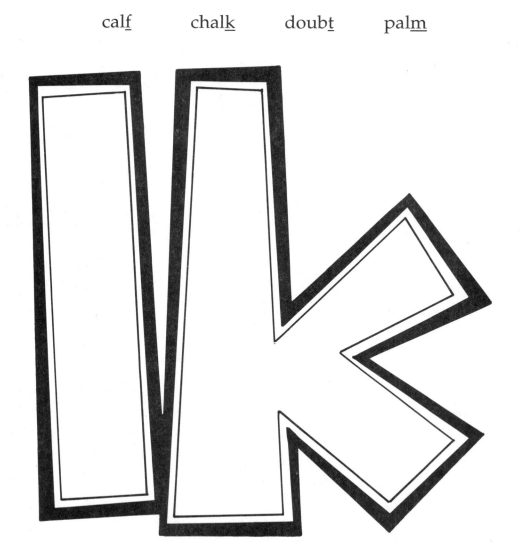

Double Consonant Sounds

When a word contains a double consonant, the first consonant is usually sounded and the second one is silent.

babble	funny	rabbit
bottle	galley	sassy
daddy	hitting	silly
error	little	sorry
gallant	minnow	taffy

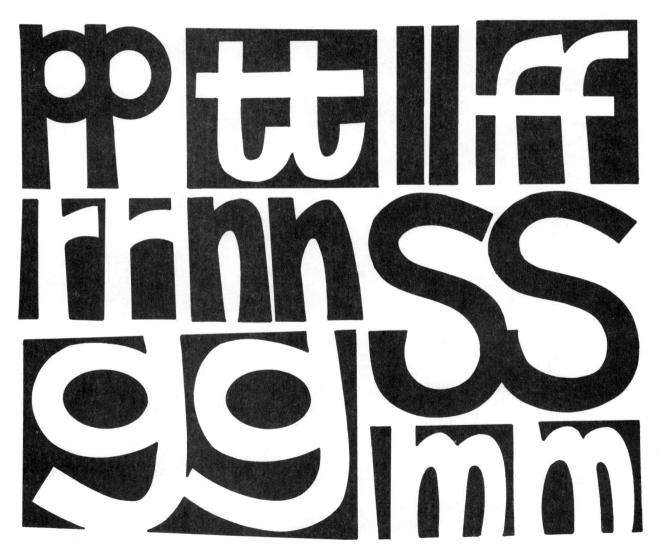

17

Consonant Sounds of S

The letter **s** can have three different sounds.

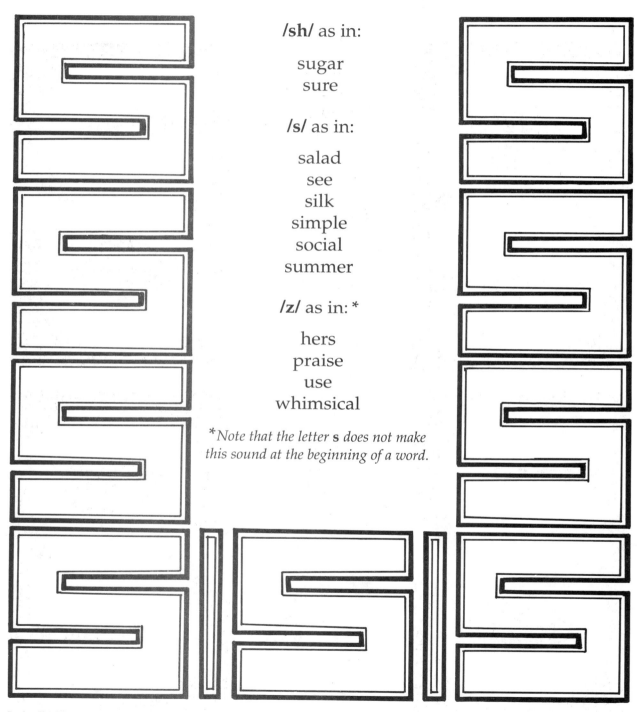

/sh/ as in:

sugar
sure

/s/ as in:

salad
see
silk
simple
social
summer

/z/ as in: *

hers
praise
use
whimsical

*Note that the letter **s** does not make this sound at the beginning of a word.*

Consonant Sounds of Qu

The letters **qu** have two different sounds.

/k/ as in:

antique
bouquet
boutique
conquer
croquet
grotesque
opaque
physique
picturesque
plaque
technique
unique

/kw/ as in:

aquarium
equal
equip
quaint
quake
quality
queen
question
quick
quite
quota
squeeze

Fearless Phonics
© The Learning Works, Inc.

Consonant Sounds of C

The consonant **c** has two different sounds. In some words it has the hard sound of **/k/** where the **c** is followed by the vowels **a**, **o**, and **u**, or followed by another consonant.

cabbage	climb	crew
cable	clue	crow
can	code	cruel
candle	coin	cry
cap	cold	cub
car	colt	cuff
card	come	cup
care	comma	curb
carrot	concept	curl
cat	cone	curry
clam	cot	curtain
class	cow	cut
clear	crab	cute

Consonant Sounds of C

In some words the consonant **c** has the soft sound of **/s/** where the **c** is followed by the vowels **e**, **i**, and **y**.

cease	certain	civic
cedar	cider	cyberspace
ceiling	cinch	cycle
celebrate	cinema	cyclone
cement	cinnamon	cylinder
cent	circle	cymbal
center	circus	cynic
cereal	citizen	cypress
	city	

21

Consonant Sounds of G

The consonant **g** has two different sounds. In some words it has the soft sound of /j/ where the **g** is followed by the vowels **e**, **i**, and **y**.

gem	geography	giraffe
gene	geometry	gym
general	germ	gymnast
generous	gesture	gyp
genius	giant	gypsy
gentle	gin	gyrate
genuine	ginger	

In some words it has the hard sound of /g/ where the **g** is followed by the vowels **a**, **o**, and **u**, or followed by another consonant.

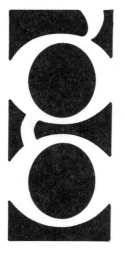

gab	glow	grew
gag	glue	grip
gain	goal	guard
gallery	gold	guess
game	golf	guide
gang	good	guitar
garden	goof	gulf
gate	gorilla	gulp
gavel	govern	gum
glare	gown	gust
glide	grand	guy

Sometimes **g** has the hard sound even when it is followed by **e** or **i**.

gecko	gift
gelding	girl
get	give

Consonant Sounds of X

The consonant **x** has three different sounds.

At the beginning of a word,
it has the sound of /**z**/.

xylem
xylophone

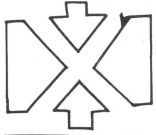

In some words it has
the sound of /**ks**/.

box
exit
explain
extra
fix
fox
hex
lox
vex

In some words it sounds
more like /**gs**/.

exact
examine
example

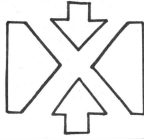
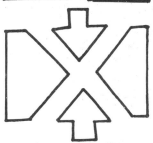

23

Fearless Phonics
© The Learning Works, Inc.

Basic Sight Words

It is extremely helpful for students to learn basic sight words—words they can pronounce in just a few seconds without having to sound out each letter. Here is a list of some common sight words.

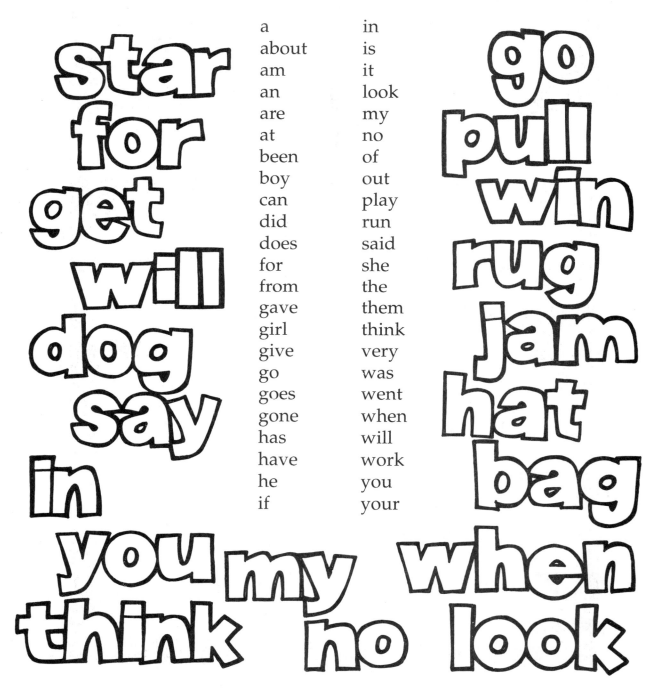

a	in
about	is
am	it
an	look
are	my
at	no
been	of
boy	out
can	play
did	run
does	said
for	she
from	the
gave	them
girl	think
give	very
go	was
goes	went
gone	when
has	will
have	work
he	you
if	your

Vowel Victories

Vowel Sounds

The vowels are **a**, **e**, **i**, **o**, **u**, and sometimes **y**.

Here are the sounds of the long and short vowels:

Long Vowel Sounds	Short Vowel Sounds
a as in ape	**a** as in am
e as in eat	**e** as in hen
i as in ice	**i** as in ink
o as in no	**o** as in pop
u as in unit	**u** as in bus
y as in my	**y** as in gym

Vowel Sounds

If **a** is the only vowel in a word or syllable, the **a** usually has the short sound of **o** when followed by **ll**, **u**, or **w**.

ball	claw	haul	mall	paw
call	hall	lawn	maul	stall

When a vowel comes before the letter **r**, the vowel has a new sound rather than a long or short sound.

are	h**ar**m	h**or**n	**ir**regular
b**ar**n	h**er**	th**or**n	**ir**ritate

27

Fearless Phonics
© The Learning Works, Inc.

Vowel Sounds

When the vowel **i** is followed by **gh**, **ld**, or **nd**, the **i** usually has a long sound.

bright	find	mind
child	light	right
fight	mild	wild

When the vowel **o** is followed by **ld**, the **o** usually has a long sound.

bold	gold	sold
cold	hold	told
fold	mold	

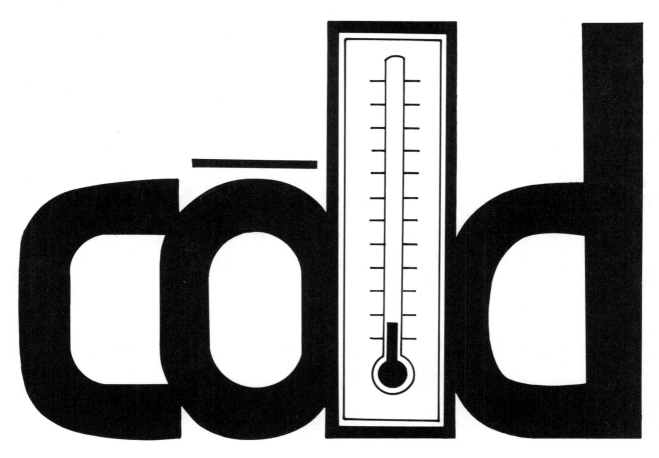

Short Vowel Sounds

back	beg	bill	bond	bug
bad	bell	bit	cost	bump
band	bent	dig	cot	cup
bat	bet	dip	dog	cut
cap	cent	fin	doll	dull
dad	desk	hid	dot	dust
fact	fed	hill	fog	fun
gasp	felt	kick	fond	gulp
hand	get	king	got	gum
hatch	help	lick	honk	hug
jam	kept	lid	job	hunt
land	let	milk	lock	jump
mask	mess	nip	lost	just
pack	nest	pig	mom	lunch
pan	peg	pink	moth	much
pat	rent	rib	not	mug
patch	sell	sink	pond	nut
sack	tent	tick	rock	punch
van	vest	wing	sob	rust
wax	well	zip	top	sun

When a word or syllable ends in a consonant, the vowel sound usually is short.

căt-tle   pĕn-ny   tĭck-le   rŏck-ing   pŭp-py

Fearless Phonics
© The Learning Works, Inc.

Short Vowel Sounds

If a word or syllable has only one vowel and it comes at the beginning of a word, the vowel usually is short.

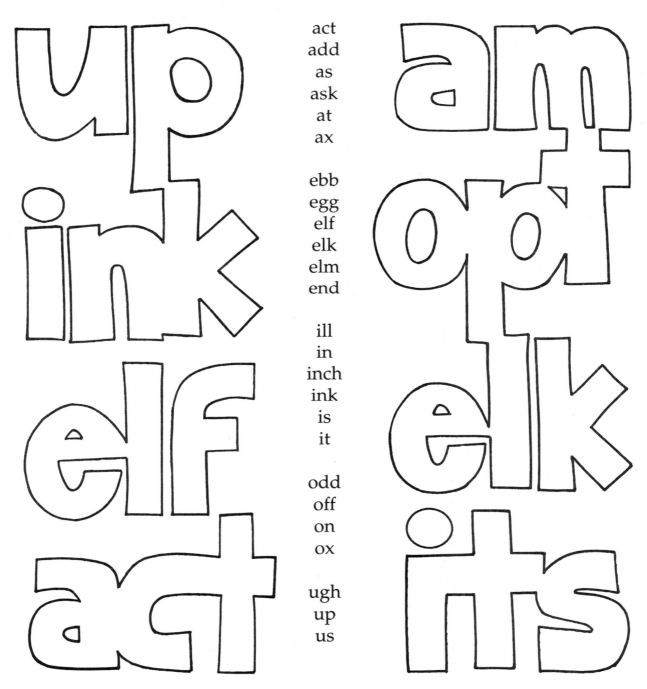

act
add
as
ask
at
ax

ebb
egg
elf
elk
elm
end

ill
in
inch
ink
is
it

odd
off
on
ox

ugh
up
us

Long Vowel Sounds

If a word has only one vowel and that vowel
appears at the end of the word, the vowel usually is long.

be	she	go	by	sky
he	we	no	fly	spy
me	hi	so	my	try

If a syllable has only one vowel, and that vowel
appears at the end of the syllable, the vowel usually is long.

ha-ven	be-cause	di-et	bro-ken	cu-bic
ra-zor	re-act	fi-nal	o-pen	u-nite

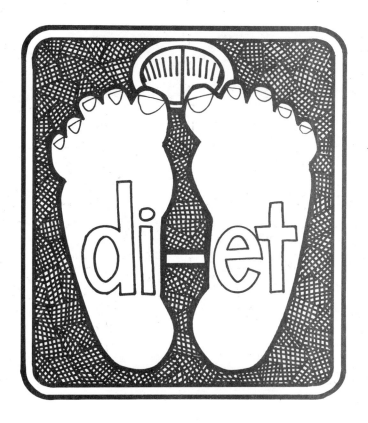

31

Fearless Phonics
© The Learning Works, Inc.

Long Vowel Sounds

If a one-syllable word has two vowels, one of which is a final **e**,
the first vowel usually is long and the final **e** is silent.

bake	cone	lake	place	rose
bike	dime	lane	plate	same
bite	dive	lime	poke	side
bone	dome	mile	pole	time
cake	fame	name	rake	tone
came	game	page	ride	use

The same rule applies to an accented syllable
that contains two vowels.

in-vādé′   pa-rādé′   sur-prīsé′

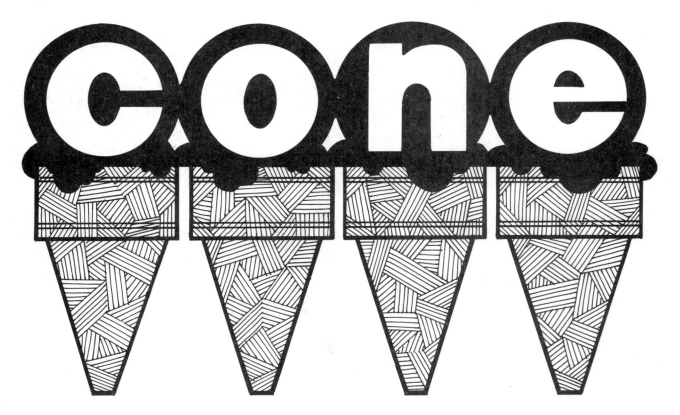

Long Vowel Sounds

If a one-syllable word has two vowels together,
the first vowel usually is long and the second is silent.

beach	dream	may	seal
bead	feed	mean	soak
beam	float	meet	stay
boat	fruit	rain	suit
clean	gain	read	team
cream	goat	road	train

33

Vowel Diphthongs

A *vowel diphthong* consists of two vowels together that have a new blended sound rather than a long or short vowel sound.

au	aw	ew	oi
auction	awe	blew	appoint
audit	bawl	brew	avoid
author	brawn	chew	boil
auto	claw	crew	broil
autumn	crawl	dew	coil
caught	dawn	drew	coin
cause	draw	few	foil
clause	drawn	flew	hoist
daughter	fawn	grew	join
fault	flaw	jewel	moist
haul	hawk	knew	noise
jaunt	jaw	mew	oil
launch	law	new	point
laundry	paw	pew	poison
maul	pawn	shrewd	soil
paunch	raw	skew	spoil
pauper	saw	slew	toil
sauce	slaw	stew	turmoil
taught	squaw	threw	voice
vault	straw	view	void

Vowel Diphthongs

A *vowel diphthong* consists of two vowels together that have a new blended sound rather than a long or short vowel sound.

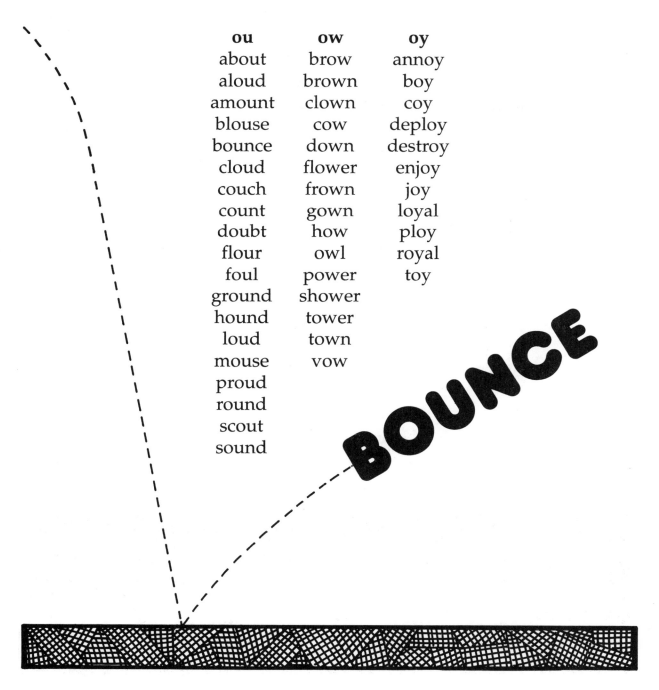

ou	ow	oy
about	brow	annoy
aloud	brown	boy
amount	clown	coy
blouse	cow	deploy
bounce	down	destroy
cloud	flower	enjoy
couch	frown	joy
count	gown	loyal
doubt	how	ploy
flour	owl	royal
foul	power	toy
ground	shower	
hound	tower	
loud	town	
mouse	vow	
proud		
round		
scout		
sound		

BOUNCE

Fearless Phonics
© The Learning Works, Inc.

Vowel Digraphs

When the letter **o** is doubled, it can make three different sounds.

oo as in *cool*:

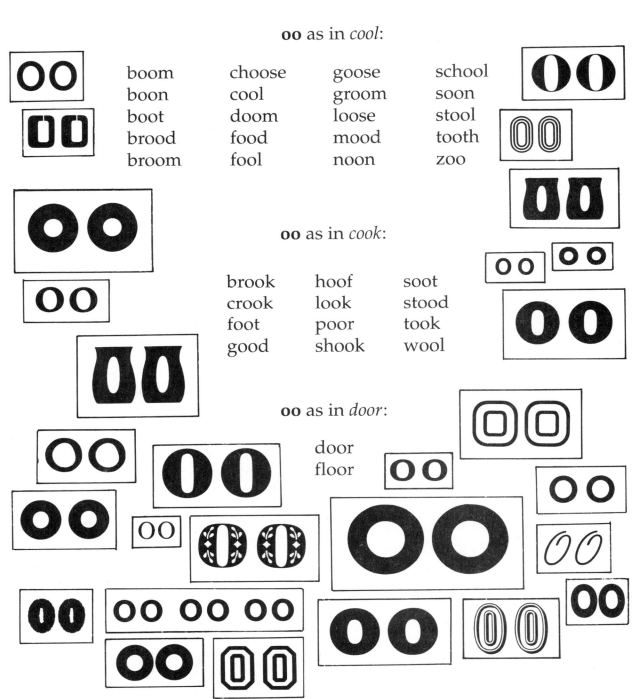

boom	choose	goose	school
boon	cool	groom	soon
boot	doom	loose	stool
brood	food	mood	tooth
broom	fool	noon	zoo

oo as in *cook*:

brook	hoof	soot
crook	look	stood
foot	poor	took
good	shook	wool

oo as in *door*:

door
floor

The Schwa

The *schwa* (ə), pronounced "shwah", is a pronunciation symbol that looks like an upside-down **e**. It stands for any vowel that is spoken softly. It is a vowel sound that usually is heard in the unaccented syllable of a word. It sounds more like a short **u** than the true sound of the vowel.

a	<u>a</u>-glow'
e	cel'-<u>e</u>-brate
i	gal'- l<u>i</u>v-ant
o	c<u>o</u>n-trol'
u	cir'-c<u>u</u>s

GORILL<u>A</u>

RHINOC<u>E</u>R<u>O</u>S

LI<u>O</u>N

CAM<u>E</u>L

HIPPOPOT<u>A</u>M<u>U</u>S

ZEBR<u>A</u>

CR<u>O</u>CODILE

Fearless Phonics
© The Learning Works, Inc.

Y Used as a Vowel

If **y** is the only vowel at the end of a one-syllable word, the **y** has a long **i** sound.

buy	dry	my	shy	spry
by	fly	ply	sky	try
cry	fry	pry	sly	why

In words with more than one syllable, the **y** has a similar sound to long **e** if the **y** is the only vowel at the end of the word.

bun-ny	glad-ly	hope-ful-ly	sil-ly
en-e-my	gra-vy	jump-y	sym-pa-thy
fun-ny	hil-ly	run-ny	ti-ny

Super Word Lists

Words With Short ă Sound

am	dad	hat	nap	sap
ant	dam	jab	pad	sat
back	fad	jam	pal	tab
bad	fan	lab	pat	tack
bag	fat	lad	ram	tag
ban	gag	lag	ran	tan
bat	gal	lamp	rap	tap
cab	gap	land	rat	van
camp	gas	mad	sack	vat
can	had	man	sad	wax
cap	ham	map	sag	yam
cat	hand	mat	sand	zag

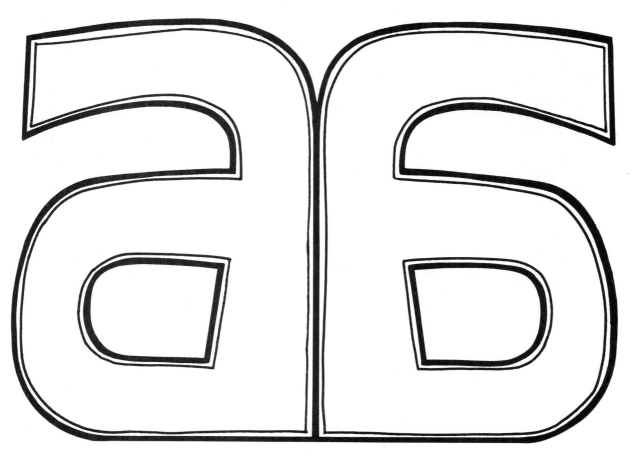

Words With Short ĕ Sound

bed	desk	kept	peg	ten
beg	fed	led	pen	vet
bell	get	leg	pet	web
best	hem	let	red	wed
bet	hen	men	rest	west
cent	jest	met	sent	wet
den	jet	net	set	yet

41

Words With Short ĭ Sound

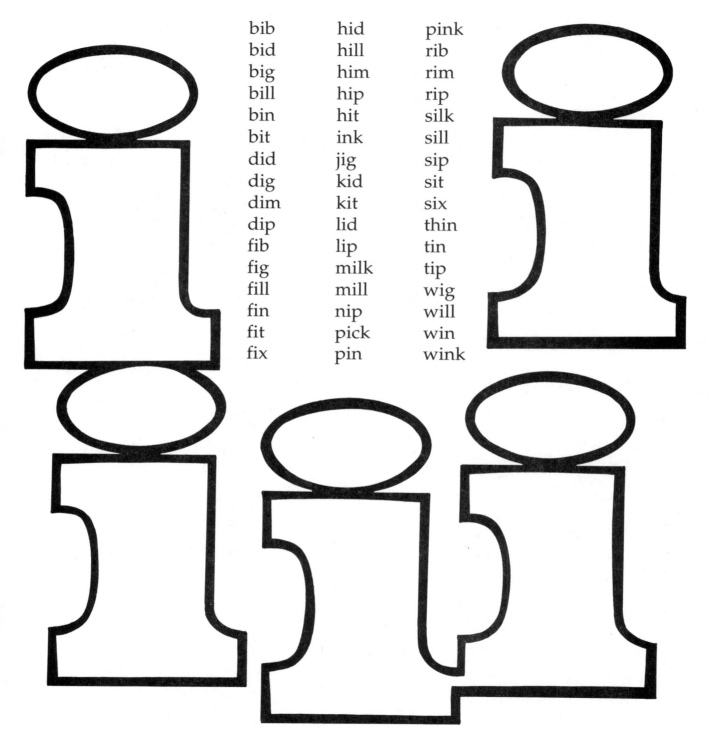

bib	hid	pink
bid	hill	rib
big	him	rim
bill	hip	rip
bin	hit	silk
bit	ink	sill
did	jig	sip
dig	kid	sit
dim	kit	six
dip	lid	thin
fib	lip	tin
fig	milk	tip
fill	mill	wig
fin	nip	will
fit	pick	win
fix	pin	wink

Words With Short ŏ Sound

bob	jot
bog	log
box	lot
cob	mob
cog	mom
cop	mop
cot	not
dog	pod
dot	pop
fog	pot
fox	rock
got	rod
hog	rot
hop	sob
hot	sock
job	sod
jog	top

43

Words With Short ŭ Sound

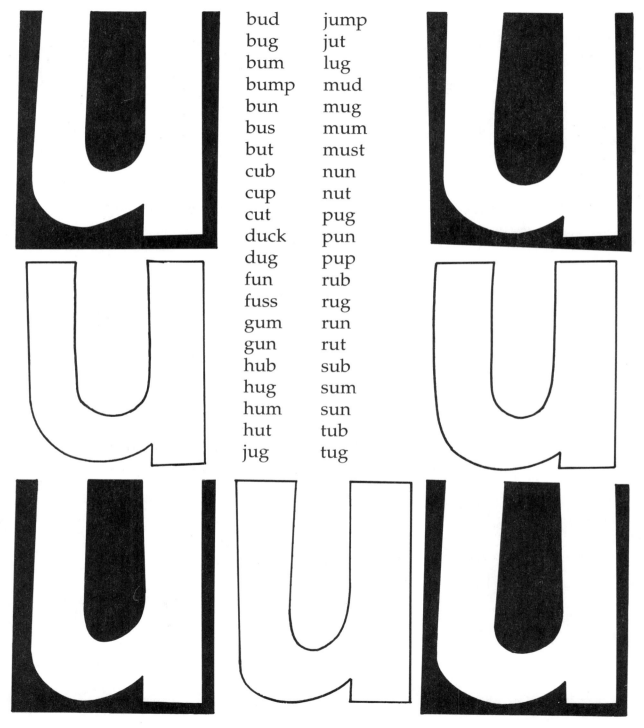

bud	jump
bug	jut
bum	lug
bump	mud
bun	mug
bus	mum
but	must
cub	nun
cup	nut
cut	pug
duck	pun
dug	pup
fun	rub
fuss	rug
gum	run
gun	rut
hub	sub
hug	sum
hum	sun
hut	tub
jug	tug

Words With Long ā Sound

ape	brave	date	flake	haste	pain	say
ate	cake	day	flame	hate	pave	shape
bake	cane	eight	frame	lake	pay	sleigh
base	cape	face	freight	lame	rain	snake
baste	case	fade	game	late	rake	take
blade	cave	fake	grade	make	rate	they
blaze	crane	fame	grape	may	reign	vein
brake	dame	fate	great	nape	same	way

Fearless Phonics
© The Learning Works, Inc.

Words With Long ē Sound

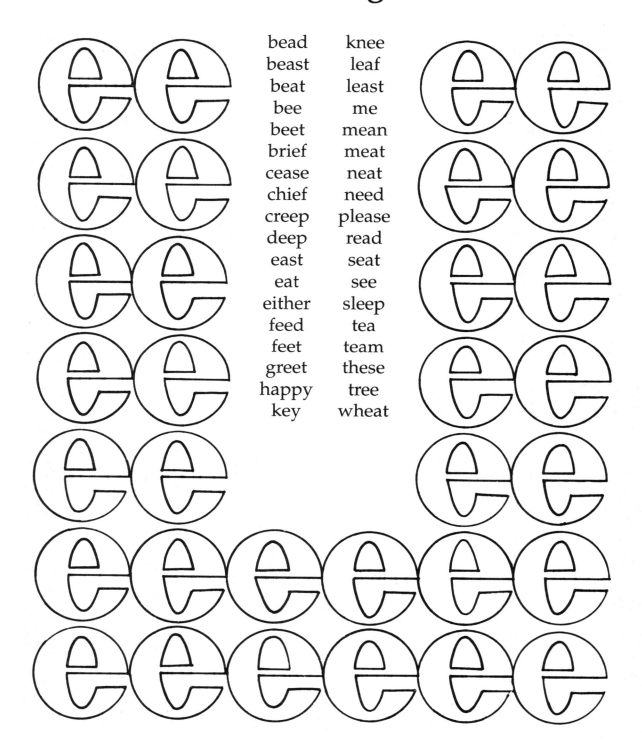

bead
beast
beat
bee
beet
brief
cease
chief
creep
deep
east
eat
either
feed
feet
greet
happy
key

knee
leaf
least
me
mean
meat
neat
need
please
read
seat
see
sleep
tea
team
these
tree
wheat

Words With Long ī Sound

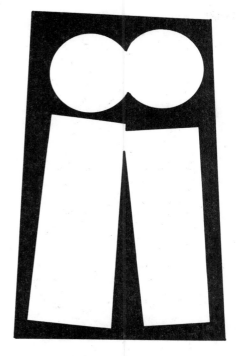

bike	mice
bite	mile
bride	mine
crime	nice
die	night
dime	pie
dine	pine
dive	pride
drive	ride
fight	right
file	side
five	slime
hide	smile
kite	tide
life	time
like	wide

Fearless Phonics
© The Learning Works, Inc.

Words With Long ō Sound

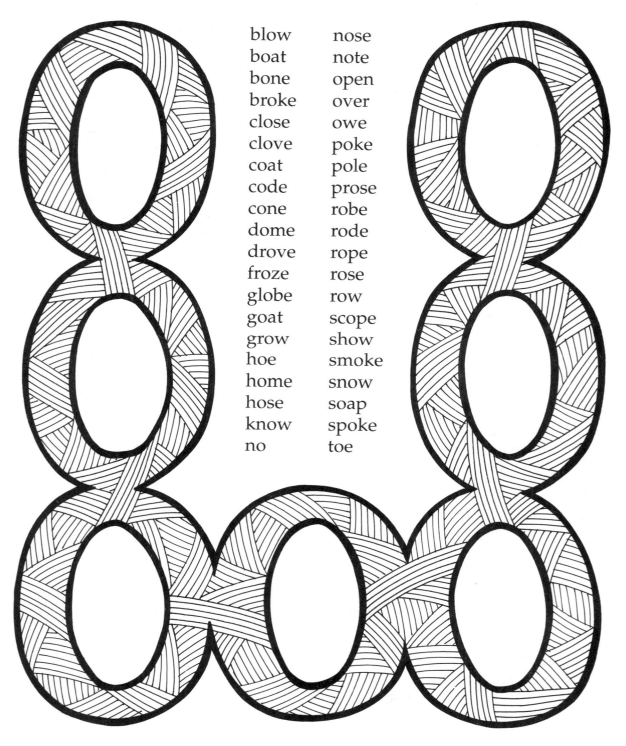

blow	nose
boat	note
bone	open
broke	over
close	owe
clove	poke
coat	pole
code	prose
cone	robe
dome	rode
drove	rope
froze	rose
globe	row
goat	scope
grow	show
hoe	smoke
home	snow
hose	soap
know	spoke
no	toe

Words With Long ū Sound

blue
bugle
crude
cube
cue
cute
dude
duke
dune
flute
hue
huge
jute
rude
true
tube
tune
unicorn
uniform
unit
use
yule

Fearless Phonics
© The Learning Works, Inc.

Rhyming Word Families

all	an	at	bag	bake
ball	ban	bat	flag	brake
call	bran	cat	gag	cake
fall	can	chat	hag	drake
gall	clan	fat	jag	fake
hall	fan	flat	lag	flake
mall	man	gnat	nag	lake
pall	pan	hat	rag	make
small	plan	mat	sag	quake
stall	ran	pat	shag	rake
tall	scan	rat	tag	sake
wall	tan	sat	wag	shake
	than	scat		snake
	van	slat		stake
		spat		take
		that		wake
		vat		

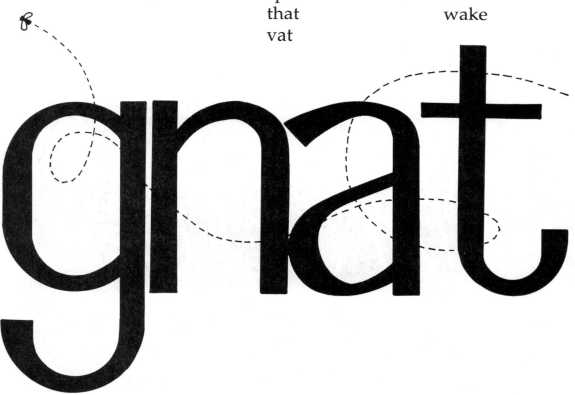

Rhyming Word Families

bank	bay	beat	bed	bend
blank	clay	cheat	bled	blend
crank	day	cleat	bred	defend
drank	fray	eat	fed	depend
flank	gay	feat	fled	end
hank	gray	heat	led	extend
plank	hay	meat	red	fend
rank	jay	neat	shed	lend
sank	lay	pleat	sled	mend
spank	may	treat	sped	send
tank	pay	wheat	wed	spend
thank	play			tend
yank	pray			trend
	ray			vend
	say			
	stay			
	sway			
	tray			
	way			

51

Fearless Phonics
© The Learning Works, Inc.

Rhyming Word Families

best	bill	bin	bit	bring
chest	chill	chin	fit	cling
crest	dill	din	flit	ding
invest	drill	fin	grit	fling
jest	fill	gin	hit	king
lest	hill	kin	it	ring
nest	kill	pin	kit	sing
pest	mill	shin	lit	sling
rest	pill	sin	mitt	spring
test	quill	skin	nit	sting
vest	skill	spin	pit	string
west	spill	thin	quit	swing
wrest	still	tin	sit	thing
zest	thrill	twin	slit	wing
	will	win	wit	

Rhyming Word Families

blot	blow	brick	bright	clear
clot	crow	chick	fight	dear
cot	flow	flick	flight	ear
dot	glow	kick	fright	fear
hot	grow	lick	knight	gear
lot	know	nick	light	hear
not	low	pick	might	near
plot	mow	quick	night	rear
pot	row	sick	right	sear
rot	show	slick	sight	shear
shot	slow	stick	slight	tear
slot	snow	thick	tight	year
spot	sow	tick		
tot	tow	trick		
trot		wick		

Fearless Phonics
© The Learning Works, Inc.

Words With Two Vowels Together

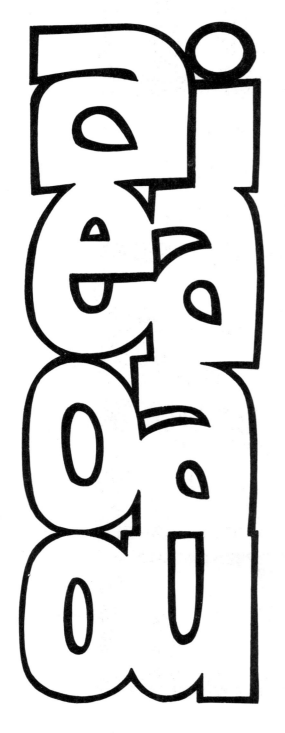

aid	drain	nail	rain
aim	fail	paid	sail
bait	gain	pail	snail
braid	grain	pain	stain
brain	hair	paint	tail
chain	maid	plain	wail
claim	mail	raid	waist

beach	dream	lead	sea
bead	each	least	seal
beak	east	meal	steal
bean	eat	meat	steam
beast	feast	peach	teach
cheap	feat	reach	team
clean	heat	read	treat
deal	jean	real	wheat

board	croak	loaf	road
boast	float	moan	roam
boat	foam	oak	roast
cloak	goad	oat	soak
coach	goal	oath	soap
coal	goat	poach	throat
coast	load	roach	toast

about	flour	house	route
cloud	ground	joust	scout
clout	hound	loud	snout
doubt	hour	mouse	wound

a·corn

Dividing Words
Into Syllables and
Placing Accent Marks

wa·ver

men·u

re·run

Dividing Words Into Syllables

A *syllable* is a group of letters that are sounded together. Each syllable must have at least one vowel sound. A word cannot have more syllables than vowel sounds.

Words pronounced as one syllable should not be divided.

carve	helped	roast
dive	learned	straight
green	patch	through

A word containing two consonants between two vowels (**vccv**) is divided between the consonants.

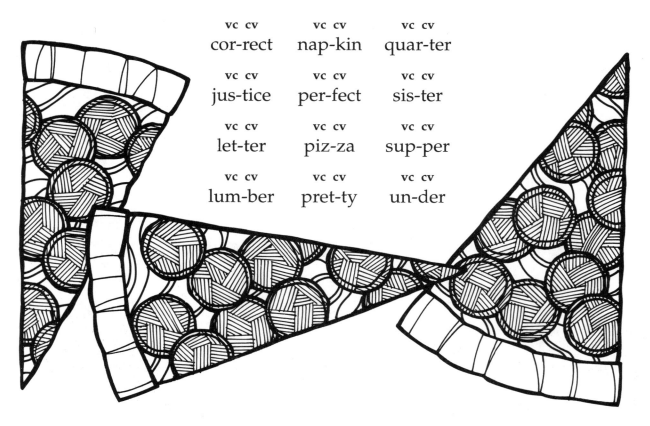

vc cv	vc cv	vc cv
cor-rect	nap-kin	quar-ter

vc cv	vc cv	vc cv
jus-tice	per-fect	sis-ter

vc cv	vc cv	vc cv
let-ter	piz-za	sup-per

vc cv	vc cv	vc cv
lum-ber	pret-ty	un-der

Dividing Words Into Syllables

In a two-syllable word containing a single consonant between two vowels (**vcv**), the consonant usually begins the second syllable.

v cv   v cv   v cv
ba-ker   mo-tion   to-day

When a prefix is added to a word, it usually forms a separate syllable.

dis-con-tent   re-cy-cle   un-hap-py

When a suffix is added to a word, it usually forms a separate syllable.

free-dom   love-ly   suc-cess-ful

Compound words usually are divided between their word parts.

air-port	inch-worm	quick-sand
bare-foot	junk-yard	rain-coat
camp-fire	key-board	sea-shore
down-stairs	lift-off	toe-nail
earth-quake	moon-light	up-right
fair-way	no-where	vine-yard
gate-house	out-fit	week-end
hair-brush	pan-cake	yard-stick

57

Dividing Words Into Syllables

In a word ending in **-le**, the consonant immediately preceding the **-le** usually begins the last syllable.

can-<u>d</u>le   mar-<u>b</u>le   ta-<u>b</u>le

Suffixes that begin with a vowel usually form separate syllables.

child-ish   dark-est   read-er

In a word containing the letter **x**, the **x** usually forms a syllable with the preceding vowel.

ex-am-ple   ex-it   ex-plain

In a word with the letters **ck**, the **ck** usually goes with the preceding vowel.

jack-et   peck-ing   tick-et

Accenting Syllables

In most two-syllable words, the first syllable usually is accented unless the word begins with a prefix.

fin'-ger   or'-der   ta'-ble

If a word begins with the prefix **a**, **be**, **de**, **in**, or **re,** that syllable usually is not accented.

a-bout'   be-hind'   de-light'   in-vest'   re-main'

In a two-syllable word containing a double consonant, the first syllable usually is accented.

hap'-py   rib'-bon   pret'-ty

In a two-syllable word where the second syllable has two vowels, the second syllable usually is accented.

de-fraud'   pre-mier'   re-ceive'

59

Accenting Syllables

In a word containing a prefix, the accent usually falls on or within the root word.

com-pose'   in-doors'   un-done'

A syllable with the letters **ck** usually is accented if it is followed by a single vowel.

jack'-et   lock'-et   pack'-et

In a compound word, the accent usually falls on or within the first word.

black'-board   court'-house   hand'-shake

In words ending in **-ical**, **-ion**, and **-ial**, the syllable preceding these endings usually is accented.

com'-i-cal   dis-cus'-sion   of-fi'-cial

Prefixes

A **prefix** is a letter or sequence of letters attached to the beginning of a word or word base.

Prefixes	Definitions	Examples
a-	in, on	abed, ashore
a-, an-	not, without	atheist, anesthetic
ab-, abs-	from, away, off	absent, absolve
alti-	high, height	altimeter, altitude
ambi-	both	ambidextrous, ambiguous
ante-	before	antecedent, antebellum
anti-	against, opposite	antifreeze, antiwar
aut-, auto-	self, same one	autograph, automobile
ben-, bene-	good, well	benediction, benefit
bi-	two, occurring every two, twice	bicycle, biweekly
biblio-	book	bibliography, bibliophile
bio-	life, living matter	biography, biology
circum-	around	circumnavigate, circumscribe
co-	with, together, joint	coauthor, coexist
contra-, contro-	against, contrary, contrasting	contradict, controversy
demi-	half	demitasse, demigod

an ambidextrous bibliophile

Fearless Phonics
© The Learning Works, Inc.

Prefixes
(continued)

Prefixes	Definitions	Examples
dis-	do the opposite of, exclude from, opposite or absence of, not	disable, disappear, disbelief
dys-	abnormal, difficult, bad	dyslexia, dystrophy
equi-	equal, equally	equidistant, equivalent
ex-	from, out of, not, former	export, extend
extra-	outside, beyond	extracurricular, extraneous
fore-	in front of, previous	forecast, forehead
geo-	earth	geography, geology
hemi-	half	hemisphere
hydro-	water	hydrofoil, hydroplane
hyper-	too much, over	hyperactive, hypersensitive
il-, im-, in-	not, without	illegal, impossible
inter-	between, among, jointly, together	interlock, interstate
intra-	within, inside	intramural, intrastate
mal-	bad, badly, abnormal, inadequate	maladjusted, malevolent

hydro hydro hydro

Prefixes

(continued)

Prefixes	Definitions	Examples
micro-	small, minute	microcosm, microphone
mis-	bad, badly, wrong, wrongly	misbehave, misprint
mono-	single, one	monologue, monorail
multi-	many, multiple, more than two	multiplex, multicolored
non-	not	nonsense, nonstop
oct-, octa-, octo-	eight	octagon, octave
orth-, ortho-	straight, upright, correct, corrective	orthodontics, orthodox
over-	above, more than is necessary, excessive, excessively	overact, overcoat
pan-	all	panacea, panorama
ped-, pedi-	foot, feet	pedal, pedicure
per-	throughout, thoroughly	perfection, pervasive
poly-	many, several, much	polygon, polyhedra
post-	after, subsequent, later	posthumous, postpone
pre-	prior to, before, in front of	prefix, preschool
pro-	earlier than, forward, in front of, taking the place of	proceed, proclaim

Fearless Phonics
© The Learning Works, Inc.

Prefixes

Prefixes	Definitions	Examples
pseud-, pseudo-	false, spurious	pseudonym, pseudomorph
re-	again, anew, back	rebound, recall
retro-	backward, back	retroactive, retrospect
se-	without, apart	select, segregate
semi-	partway, half	semiannual, semitrailer
sub-	under, beneath, below, subordinate, secondary	submarine, subtract
super-	over and above, more than, quantity or degree, higher in quantity	superior, superman
tele-	far	telescope, television
trans-	across, beyond, through	transfer, transport
tri-	three, once in every three	triangle, triplets
ultra-	beyond, extreme, extremely	ultramodern, ultraviolet
un-	not, do the opposite of, deprive of	unfinished, unlucky
uni-	one, single	unicycle, unilateral
vice-	acting for, next in rank to	vice-president, viceroy

super super super super

Suffixes

A **suffix** is a letter or sequence of letters that has a specific definition and may be added to the end of a word or word base to change its meaning.

Suffixes	Definitions	Examples
-able, -ible	capable or worthy of	changeable
-age	action or process; rate of; fee	postage
-ance, -ancy	act, process, or state of being	brilliance
-ant, -ent	one who performs a specified action	confidant
-dom	office; state or fact of being	freedom
-ence, ency	act, process, or state of being	absence
-er, -or	one who; that which	banker, editor
-ful	full of; number or quality that fills	cupful, roomful
-fy	to make; to invest with the attributes of	simplify
-hood	condition, time, or instance of	motherhood
-ion	act, condition, state, or process of	exploration
-ish	characteristic of or relating to	foolish
-ism	belief or practice of	intellectualism
-ist	one who performs a specified action; one who advocates a particular position	florist, communist
-ity, -ty, -y	quality, state, or degree of	civility
-ive	tending to	supportive, attentive

Fearless Phonics
© The Learning Works, Inc.

Suffixes
(continued)

Suffixes	Definitions	Examples
-ize	to cause to conform to; to become like	theorize, westernize
-logue, -log	speech or disclosure	monologue, dialogue
-logy	oral or written expression; doctrine, theory, or study of	biology, criminology
-ment	act, process, or state of being; concrete result of an action	entanglement, merriment
-ness	state, condition, quality, or degree of	happiness, kindness
-ory	having the quality of; being characterized by; a place or thing for	sensory, laboratory, derogatory
-osis	act, condition, or process of	metamorphosis
-ous, -ose	full of; having or possessing the qualities of	anxious, comatose
-ship	state of being; the art or skill of	friendship, kinship
-some	causing or characterized by	lonesome, worrisome
-tude	state, condition, quality, or degree of	gratitude, altitude
-ward	in the direction of	upward
-y	characterized by; full of; inclined to	dusty, sleepy

Roots and Combining Forms

A **root** is the simple element from which a more complex word is derived, often by means of the addition of prefixes, suffixes, and/or other combining forms.

Roots	Definitions	Examples
act	do	action
-agogue	leader	demagogue
agr-	field	agriculture
altus, alte	high	altitude
alter	other (of two)	alternate
annus, anno	year	annual
anthrop-, anthropo-, -anthrop	human being, man	misanthrope
aqui-, aqua-	water	aquatic
arch-	chief, principal	archangel
-archy	rule, government	anarchy
astr-, astro-	star	astronomy
brevi-	short	abbreviation
cand	white, bright, shining	incandescent, candle
captus	take, seize, hold	capture
caput, capitis	head	cap, capital, decapitate

action · anarchy · annual · anthropology

Fearless Phonics
© The Learning Works, Inc.

Roots and Combining Forms

(continued)

Roots	Definitions	Examples
cent	hundred	century, percent
chron-, chrono-	time	chronological
citare	put in motion; summon	citation
clarus	clear	clarity
cogito	turn over in the mind; think	cogitate
cogna-, cogni-	know	recognize
cosm-, cosmo-, -cosm	order, world	cosmopolitan
cred-	believe	incredible
culpa	blame, guilt	culprit
cycle	circle, ring, wheel	bicycle
derm-, derma, -derm	skin	epidermis
dict-	say, speak	diction, edict
doc-, doct-	instruct, teach	docent, doctor
dominus	master of the house, lord, ruler	dominate

Roots and Combining Forms
(continued)

Roots	Definitions	Examples
flex	bend	flexible
flor, flora	flower	floral, florist
flux	flow	influx
fort	strong	fortify
fragilis	fragile; easily broken	fragile
fus-	pour, melt	fusion
-gon	angle	polygon
-gram	drawing, writing	telegram
gratus	pleasing, thankful	gratitude, gratuitous
greg-	of or relating to a crowd, flock, or herd	segregate, gregarious
hem-, hema-, hemo-	blood	hemorrhage
hydr-, hydro-	water	hydrofoil
iacto	to throw, cast, or fling away	eject, interject
is-, iso-	equal, homogeneous	isometric
liber	to free	liberate

Fearless Phonics
© The Learning Works, Inc.

Roots and Combining Forms

(continued)

Roots	Definitions	Examples
locus	a single place	location
logos, logi	word, words	monologue
magnus	great, large	magnify, magnitude
manus	the hand	manufacture
mare	the sea	marine, maritime
mega-	great, large	megaphone
mitto, mittere	to send or dispatch	remit, transmit
mobilito	to set in motion	mobilize
navigo	to sail	navigate
ne-, neo-	new	neoclassic
nego, negare	to say no	negate, negative
-nomy	system of laws governing or knowledge regarding	astronomy, autonomy
novus	fresh, new, young, inexperienced	novel, novice
ocul-, oculo-	having to do with the eyes	binoculars, ocular
pan-	all	panorama

Roots and Combining Forms
(continued)

Roots	Definitions	Examples
paed-, ped-	child	pediatrics
phil-, philo-	loving; having an affinity for	philanthropist
phon-, phono-	sound, voice, speech	phonograph
phot-, photo-	light	photography, photon
porto, portare	to bear, bring, or carry	portable, transport
prior, primus	former, first	primary
psych-, psycho-	brain, mind, spirit	psychic
pyr-, pyro-	fire, heat	pyromania
rogo, rogare	to ask or question	interrogate
rumpere, ruptum	to break or shatter	interrupt, erupt
scribere, scriptum	to write	prescribe, script
secare, sectum	to cut	dissect, intersection
solus, soli	alone, only	solely, solitary
somnus	sleep, slumber	insomnia
sono, sonare	to sound or make a noise	sonorous, resonant

intersection

Fearless Phonics
© The Learning Works, Inc.

Roots and Combining Forms

(continued)

Roots	Definitions	Examples
struo, struere, structum	to put together; to build	construct, structure
techno-	art, craft, skill	technique
tempus, temporis	a period of time	contemporary
tenuo, tenuare	to make thin, fine, or slender	tenuous
termino, terminare	to bound, limit, or make an end to	terminate
terra	earth, land	terrain, terrarium
testor, testare	to bear witness to; to give evidence of	testify
therm-, thermo-	heat	thermometer
torquare, tortum	to twist, wind, or wrench	contort, distort
tribuere, tributum	to divide out; to assign, give, or pay to	tribute
turbo, turbare	to agitate; to throw into disorder or confusion	disturb, turbulence